DIRT BIKE CRAZY

KTM DIRT BIKES

By R. L. Van

Kaleidoscope
Minneapolis, MN

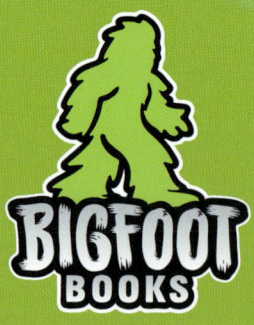

The Quest for Discovery Never Ends

....

This edition is co-published by agreement between Kaleidoscope and World Book, Inc.

Kaleidoscope Publishing, Inc.
6012 Blue Circle Drive
Minnetonka, MN 55343 U.S.A.

World Book, Inc.
180 North LaSalle St., Suite 900
Chicago IL 60601 U.S.A.

All rights reserved. No part of this book may be reproduced in any form without written permission from the publishers.

Kaleidoscope ISBNs
978-1-64519-093-6 (library bound)
978-1-64494-154-6 (paperback)
978-1-64519-197-1 (ebook)

World Book ISBN
978-0-7166-4366-1 (library bound)

Library of Congress Control Number
2019939019

Text copyright ©2020 by Kaleidoscope Publishing, Inc. All-Star Sports, Bigfoot Books, and associated logos are trademarks and/or registered trademarks of Kaleidoscope Publishing, Inc.

Printed in the United States of America.

Bigfoot lurks within one of the images in this book. It's up to you to find him!

TABLE OF CONTENTS

Chapter 1: KTM in Action **4**

Chapter 2: Ready to Race **10**

Chapter 3: Choosing a Champion **16**

Chapter 4: Wearing Orange **22**

    Beyond the Book 28

    Research Ninja 29

    Further Resources 30

    Glossary 31

    Index 32

    Photo Credits 32

    About the Author 32

CHAPTER 1

KTM in Action

Pierce is at the starting line. Trees tower over him. It's a cool, overcast day. It might rain. Pierce puts down the visor on his helmet. He waits for the race to begin.

Pierce rides a KTM 250 XC-F dirt bike. The front fender is traffic-cone orange. Orange decals accent the seat. Behind Pierce, the body tapers to a point. The bike looks like an arrow.

KTM designed Pierce's bike for enduro. Enduro is an off-road dirt bike race. Some enduro races are 150 miles (241 km) long. Bikers race in groups. Fewer bikes crowd the trail this way. The flag drops. Pierce speeds off.

FUN FACT
The 250 XC-F can go over 90 miles per hour (145 km/h)!

The KTM 250 XC-F is an enduro bike.

The trail is rough. Pierce holds the handlebars tightly. Some riders bounce around. But Pierce's ride is much smoother. His bike's **suspension** can handle this trail.

Pierce drives through the woods. He loves feeling the wind on his face. He likes the smell of the mud. His tires have big knobs in them. These knobs help grip the mud. On some bikes, mud clogs the **transmission**. But the KTM 250 XC-F is different. It has a "No Dirt" gear-shift lever. Mud can't clog the lever's joint as easily. The transmission shifts gears smoothly.

Kacy Martinez raced her 250 XC-F on the KTM Factory Racing Team until her retirement in 2018.

PARTS OF A
KTM 250 XC-F

Mud still makes the ground slippery. Pierce sees mud puddles ahead. He uses the **traction** control setting. He flips a switch on the handlebar. This gives him more control on the wet ground. One wheel might start spinning faster than the other. The traction control senses this. It puts the brakes on the faster wheel. The bike stays steady.

The race is close. Pierce wants to reach the checkpoint first. He will have to be fast. Luckily, the KTM 250 XC-F is small. It's smaller than most enduro bikes. It also has lighter wheels and a lighter engine. This helps make it faster. Pierce pulls ahead of the other riders. He reaches the checkpoint first. Yes! He pumps his fist. But the day isn't over yet. He still has many miles to go.

Enduro races are one of the oldest types of motorcycle competitions.

CHAPTER 2

Ready to Race

It was 1954. Hans Trunkenpolz was ready to race. He was the founder of KTM. *KTM* stands for Kronreif Trunkenpolz Mattighofen. He named the company after himself and his assistant. His assistant was Ernst Kronreif. Mattighofen was their town in Austria. KTM had recently made the R125 Tourist.

Trunkenpolz raced the R125 Tourist from Paris to Vienna. This got the public's attention.

It was bigger and faster than its first model. It could go 56 miles per hour (90 km/h). Trunkenpolz wanted to show it off. So he went to Paris. He and two other riders were going to race. They all rode R125 Tourists. But they weren't going to race each other. They were going to race a train.

KTM bikes have come a long way since 1954.

The Arlberg Express train ran from Paris to Vienna. It would be an 808-mile (1,300-km) ride. The trip usually took twenty-four hours by train. Trunkenpolz knew his bike could keep up. The train started to move. The riders kick-started their bikes.

The R125 Tourist was different from KTM bikes today. It was not as advanced. The riders had to race at full **throttle**. The bikes' headlights were weak. The **fork** leg on Trunkenpolz's bike broke. But they made it to Vienna. They arrived two hours before the train. They proved the bike's speed and **reliability**.

OUT-OF-STYLE ORANGE

In 1990, KTM held a contest. KTM was looking for a head designer. George Kiska won. He was now in charge of choosing how the bikes looked. This included the color. He chose orange for the company. In the 1990s, orange was not a stylish color. But that's what made people notice it. Orange popped.

13

KTM has continued to **innovate** ever since. In 1992, it built an EXC bike. It was designed for enduro racing. KTM says that enduro is the heart of its company. KTM is proud of the EXC's success. KTM also makes motocross, rally, and other off-road bikes.

KTM started making something new in 2015. It's an electric dirt bike. It's called the FREERIDE E-XC. It zooms around city roads and rough trails. But KTM doesn't just make dirt bikes. Its motorcycles and sports cars are sleek. They zip by the competition on the racetrack. KTM makes something for everyone.

FUN FACT
KTM makes a sports car called the X-Bow.

The FREERIDE E-XC is KTM's first electric dirt bike.

CHAPTER 3

Choosing a Champion

Jacob climbs onto his KTM 450 SX-F. It looks like most other KTM bikes. It has an orange-and-white body. The ends are pointed. But this bike is special. This is the model that MXGP world champions ride. MXGP stands for Motocross Grand Prix. Jeffrey Herlings and Tony Cairoli are MXGP riders. They both race on this bike. Jacob would like to compete with them one day. He'll start by winning this race.

The race starts. Jacob speeds ahead. Jacob's engine makes a deep roaring sound. Up ahead, there is a sharp turn. The 450 SX-F handles this without trouble. It has a balanced suspension. It's easy to move. It's the lightest dirt bike in its **class**. All of this helps the bike handle sharp turns.

Jacob reaches a straight part of the track. It has many hills in a row. The bike handles these waves easily. Its **shock absorbers** and air fork reduce the impact. Most dirt bikes have forks with springs in them. But KTM uses air forks in most of its bikes.

FUN FACT
The KTM 450 SX-F is KTM's fastest motocross bike.

The 450 SX-F is a good option for motocross racers.

KTM's air forks have two parts. One is filled with air. The air pressure absorbs shock. The other part is called a balance chamber. It adjusts the air pressure in the fork. Riders can easily make changes. They can set it up for the track.

The air fork works for Jacob. Spring forks are heavier. Jacob's bike isn't weighed down. He jumps over the last hill. His tire gets back to the ground more quickly than the others'. He can speed up before they can. He pulls ahead of the other riders. He's going to win the race.

BIKE MODEL	250 XC-F	450 SX-F	FREERIDE E-XC NG
SUITABLE FOR	Enduro	Motocross	Off-road
ENGINE SIZE	250cc	450cc	N/A
ENGINE TYPE	Two-stroke	Four-stroke	E-motor
TRANSMISSION	Six-speed	Four-speed	Single-speed
BASE PRICE	$9,499	$9,899	$8,299

COMPARE AND CONTRAST
KTM DIRT BIKES

250 XC-F

450 SX-F

FREERIDE E-XC NG

Jacob's little sister Leah rides dirt bikes, too. She loves riding on mountain trails. She drives by shimmering creeks. She loves nature. She chose the KTM FREERIDE E-XC.

The FREERIDE E-XC is electric. It doesn't use fuel. It doesn't pollute the air. And it's much quieter than her brother's bike. It makes a high whining noise, not a roar. The bike has great suspension. This helps her drive on bumpy trails. The bike's battery can last up to one and a half hours. It also has lights, turn signals, and mirrors. This means Leah can drive it on regular streets.

The FREERIDE E-XC is great for riders who love nature.

Waves are a common motocross obstacle.

FUN FACT
Once the battery gets below 10%, the FREERIDE starts "limp home mode."

CHAPTER 4

By 2019, Jeffrey Herlings had four world championships and eighty-four Grand Prix wins.

Wearing Orange

Motocross champions often ride KTM. Jeffrey Herlings is from the Netherlands. He rides MXGP for KTM. He struggled in 2017. It was his first year racing in the 450 class. He broke his hand before the first race. He was used to winning. But suddenly he was falling behind. He was losing confidence.

FUN FACT
Jeffrey Herlings's nickname is "The Bullet."

Herlings trained harder for the next season. The 2018 KTM 450 SX-F had some updates. He got to test it out early. He was impressed. The engine and steering felt better for him. His hard work paid off. So did the new bike. He was the 2018 MXGP world champion.

Josh Toth was twenty-one when he started riding for KTM.

KTM also has champions in off-road races like enduro. American Josh Toth rides a KTM 250 XC-F. Growing up, he and his brothers had to share a bike. After high school, he was learning to be a plumber. He saved up money to race. His boss let him take time off to compete. Soon, he got an offer to race professionally. He joined KTM's 2018 team.

Toth races in the National Enduro Series. His years of practice helped him in 2018. So did his KTM bike. He got second place. First, third, and fourth places also went to KTM riders.

KTM has many racers on its Factory Racing Team. Like Herlings and Toth, these racers win. This is because KTM bikes are some of the best. Riders using KTM bikes have won more than 270 world championship titles. Thanks to KTM, they are ready to race.

KTM riders win many races.

Red Bull
KTM
MOTOREX
PIRELLI
Red Bull
KTM
MXGP of Trentino
MX2 CLASS
KTM

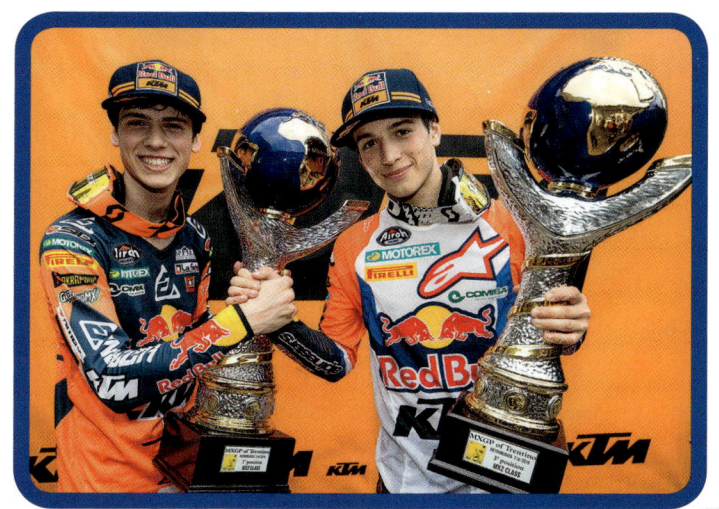

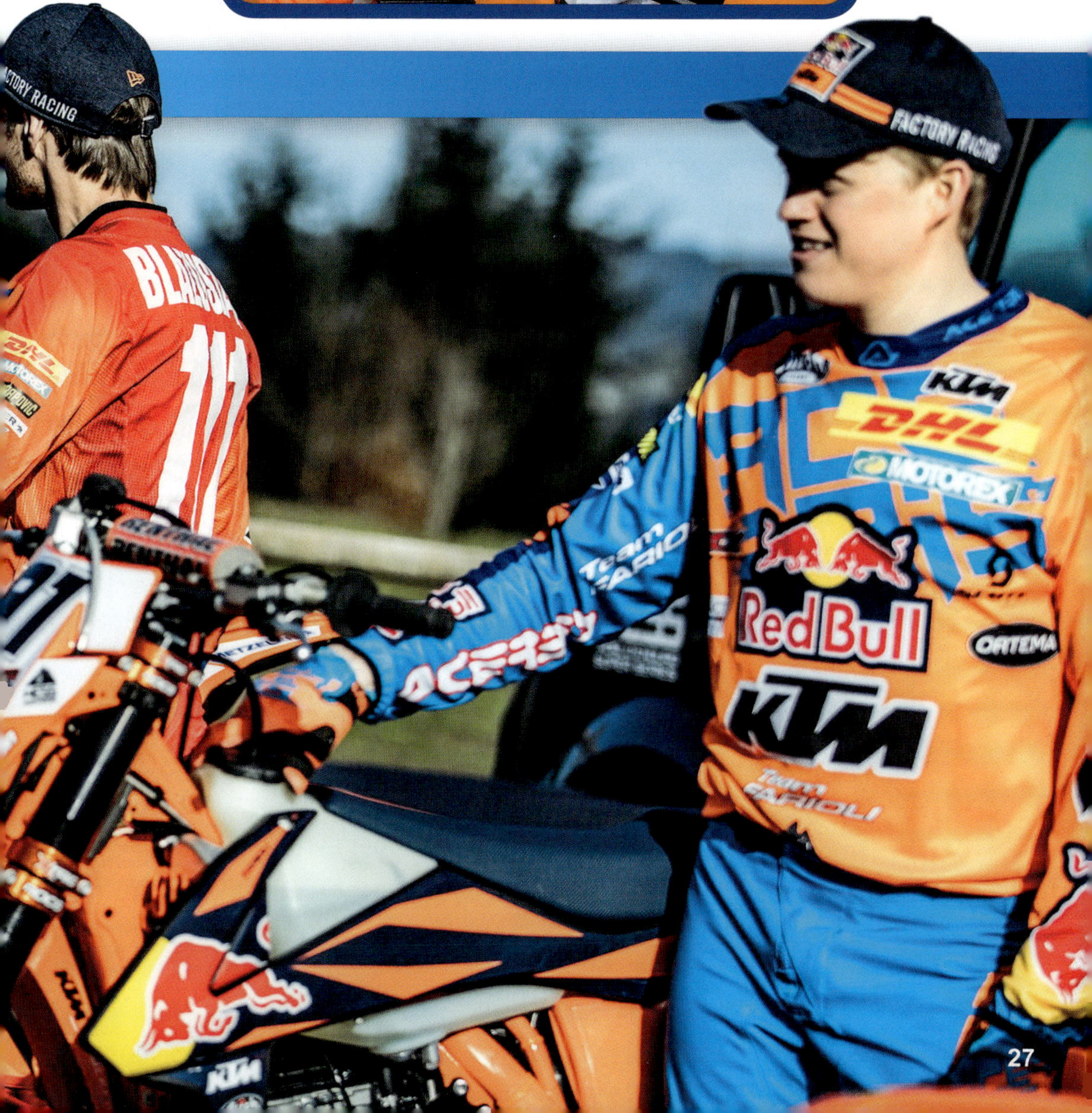
FACTORY RACING
FACTORY RACING
KTM
DHL
MOTOREX
Red Bull
ORTEMA
KTM
Team FARIOLI
KTM

BEYOND THE BOOK

After reading the book, it's time to think about what you learned. Try the following exercises to jumpstart your ideas.

THINK

THAT'S NEWS TO ME. Jeffrey Herlings won the 2018 MXGP FIM Motocross World Championship. How might news sources be able to fill in more detail about this? What new information could you find in news articles? Where could you go to find those sources?

CREATE

SHARPEN YOUR RESEARCH SKILLS. KTM's FREERIDE E-XC electric dirt bike was developed in 2015. It's very different from standard dirt bikes. Where could you go in the library to learn more about electric dirt bikes? Who could you talk to who might know more? Create a research plan. Write a paragraph about your next steps.

SHARE

WHAT'S YOUR OPINION? The text states that KTM bikes are some of the best. Do you agree or disagree with this position? Use evidence from the text to support your answer. Share your position and evidence with a friend. Does your friend agree with you?

GROW

REAL-LIFE RESEARCH. What places could you visit to learn more about KTM dirt bikes? What other things could you learn while you were there?

RESEARCH NINJA

Visit www.ninjaresearcher.com/0936 to learn how to take your research skills and book report writing to the next level!

RESEARCH

DIGITAL LITERACY TOOLS

SEARCH LIKE A PRO
Learn about how to use search engines to find useful websites.

FACT OR FAKE?
Discover how you can tell a trusted website from an untrustworthy resource.

TEXT DETECTIVE
Explore how to zero in on the information you need most.

SHOW YOUR WORK
Research responsibly—learn how to cite sources.

WRITE

GET TO THE POINT
Learn how to express your main ideas.

PLAN OF ATTACK
Learn prewriting exercises and create an outline.

DOWNLOADABLE REPORT FORMS

Further Resources

BOOKS

Abdo, Kenny. *Dirt Bikes.* Abdo Publishing, 2018.

Lanier, Wendy Hinote. *Dirt Bikes.* Focus Readers, 2017.

Shaffer, Lindsay. *Dirt Bikes.* Bellwether Media, 2019.

WEBSITES

FACTSURFER

Factsurfer.com gives you a safe, fun way to find more information.

1. Go to www.factsurfer.com.
2. Enter "KTM Dirt Bikes" into the search box and click 🔍.
3. Select your book cover to see a list of related websites.

Glossary

class: A class is a set of things that have something in common. Bikes in the 450 class have 450cc engines.

fork: A fork connects the bike's frame to its front wheel and provides suspension. A fork often has springs inside to absorb shock, but KTM bikes have air forks.

innovate: To innovate means to do something in a new way. KTM continues to innovate, making its bikes better every year.

reliability: Something has reliability if you can count on it to perform well. The R125 demonstrated its reliability by driving well in a race that lasted almost twenty-four hours.

shock absorbers: Shock absorbers absorb impact to provide a smoother ride. The shock absorbers on the KTM FREERIDE E-XC keep riders comfortable even on bumpy, rocky roads.

suspension: A vehicle's suspension system keeps it steady over obstacles and absorbs shock. The KTM 450 SX-F dirt bike has air forks to provide front suspension.

throttle: A throttle is a device that allows riders to control how much power goes to the engine. When someone rides a dirt bike full throttle, that rider is using as much power as possible.

traction: Traction is the ability of tires to grip the ground. Jeffrey Herlings's tires had excellent traction, so his bike gripped the ground through the loose dirt.

transmission: The transmission is the system that shifts gears or changes speed on a dirt bike. The "No-Dirt" lever in a KTM bike's transmission doesn't get clogged with dirt, so it can change gears even in muddy conditions.

Index

250 XC-F, 4–9, 18–19, 25
450 SX-F, 16, 18–19, 23

air forks, 8, 16–18
Austria, 10, 13

Cairoli, Tony, 16

enduro, 4–9, 14, 18, 25

Factory Racing Team, 22–26
FREERIDE E-XC, 14, 18–19, 20, 21

Herlings, Jeffrey, 16, 22–23, 26

Kiska, George, 13

motocross, 14, 16, 18, 22–23
mud, 6, 9

orange, 4, 13, 16

R125 Tourist, 10–13

suspension, 6, 16, 20

Toth, Josh, 25–26
traction control, 9
trains, 11–13
transmission, 6, 18
Trunkenpolz, Hans, 10–13

X-Bow, 14

PHOTO CREDITS

The images in this book are reproduced through the courtesy of: smileimage9/Shutterstock Images, front cover; KTM, pp. 3, 4–5, 8, 10–11, 11, 13, 15, 16–17, 19 (top), 19 (middle), 19 (bottom), 20, 21 (top), 21 (bottom), 30; Simon Cudby/KTM, pp. 6–7, 9, 22–23, 24–25; Swijgers B./KTM, pp. 12–13; Kernasenko J./KTM, p. 14; Red Line Editorial, pp. 18–19; Ray Archer/KTM, pp. 23, 27; Hill K./KTM, p. 25; Marcin Kin/KTM, pp. 26–27.

ABOUT THE AUTHOR

R. L. Van is a writer and editor from Minnesota. She loves reading, animals, and crossword puzzles.